# Macroeconomics and Fiscal Policy

Roggie Clark

# Continue Learning At Our Website: Roggieclarkbooks.com

Continue exploring educational resources, tools, books, workbooks, and learning materials designed to help readers continue building knowledge and practical skills. Visit: www.roggieclarkbooks.com

Inside you'll find:

- Educational worksheets
- Beginner-friendly guides
- Printable activities
- Companion materials for books and courses

A growing library of educational content for readers, collectors, learners, parents, teachers, and lifelong students.

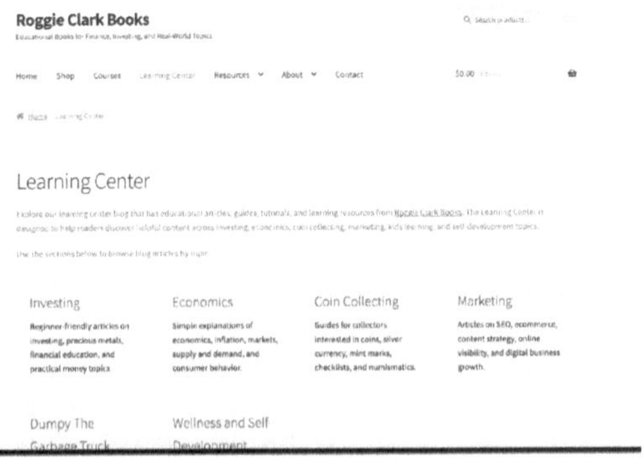

## Learn Macro and Micro Economics, With This One Book

Whether you're a student, a professional, or simply someone eager to understand the world around you, this book is your perfect introduction to the fundamentals of micro and macroeconomics.

https://www.amazon.com/Macro-Micro-Economics-Workbook-Beginners-ebook/dp/B0FVPMFX6B

# The Strategic Guide to U.S. Mint Gold and Silver Coin Investing

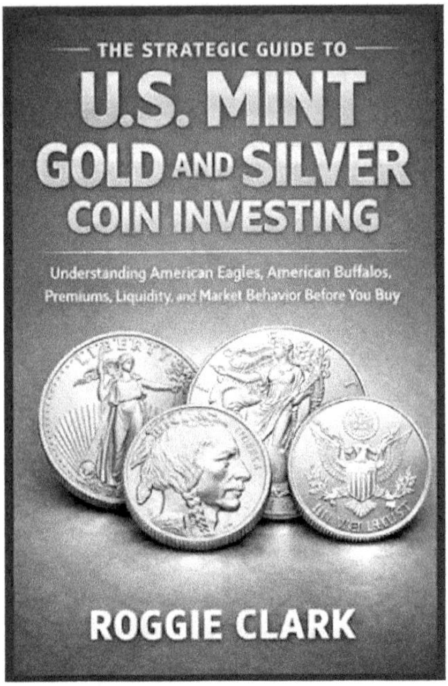


Rather than offering a general introduction to precious metals, this guide examines how American Gold Eagles, American Gold Buffalos, and Silver American Eagles behave in real investor markets.

https://www.amazon.com/Strategic-Guide-U-S-Silver-Investing/dp/B0GQKJF9K6

# Copyright

Title: Macroeconomics and Fiscal Policy
Author: Roggie Clark



Cover Design: Roggie Clark
Editing: Renee' Clark

Printed in the United States of America

# Disclaimer

The views and opinions expressed in this publication are those of the author and do not necessarily reflect the official policies, positions, opinions, or viewpoints of any individual, company, organization, institution, agency, or entity referenced or mentioned within this work.

The author is not necessarily affiliated with, endorsed by, sponsored by, or compensated by any individuals, companies, organizations, brands, institutions, products, or services referenced within this publication unless specifically stated otherwise. Any examples, sample situations, stories, illustrations, or scenarios presented may be fictionalized or simplified for educational purposes. Any resemblance to actual persons, living or dead, businesses, or events is purely coincidental unless otherwise stated.

The information, ideas, strategies, concepts, techniques, opinions, suggestions, and educational materials contained in this publication are provided on an "as is" basis without warranties of any kind, either express or implied. While every effort has been made to provide accurate and current information, neither the author nor the publisher makes any representations or warranties regarding the completeness, accuracy, reliability, suitability, or applicability of the information presented.

This publication is intended solely for educational and informational purposes and should not be interpreted as professional advice of any kind, including but not limited to financial, investment, legal, tax, business, medical, mental health, educational, psychological, or other professional guidance. Readers should conduct their own independent research and consult appropriately qualified professionals before making decisions that may affect their finances, health, business, education, legal matters, personal circumstances, or other important areas of life.

Results, outcomes, and experiences may vary significantly among individuals. Neither the author nor the publisher guarantees any specific outcomes, results, earnings, performance improvements, personal achievements, or benefits resulting from the use of information contained in this publication.

By reading, accessing, or using this publication, you acknowledge and agree that the author and publisher shall not be held liable for any direct, indirect, incidental, consequential, financial, personal, emotional, or other damages, losses, or claims arising from the use, misuse, interpretation, or application of information contained within this publication. You assume full responsibility for any actions, decisions, and outcomes resulting from the use of this material.

# Image Credits and Public Domain Notice

All images, illustrations, graphics, photographs, visual references, and related materials included in this publication are believed to be in the public domain, used under applicable licenses or permissions, created by the author or publisher, or obtained from sources that clearly identify them as available for lawful use.

The author and publisher have made a good faith effort to use only visual materials that are lawfully available for use and distribution. Where applicable, images and visual materials may have been resized, cropped, edited, enhanced, stylized, modified, reformatted, or arranged for educational, informational, design, formatting, or presentation purposes.

This publication is intended for educational, informational, and illustrative purposes only. The inclusion of any image, artwork, photograph, visual reference, symbol, historical material, design, or graphic element is not intended to claim ownership over public domain materials or any third-party intellectual property rights that remain with their respective owners.

If you believe any image or visual material included in this publication has been used in error, please contact the author or publisher so the matter may be reviewed and corrected in future editions or releases if necessary.

Any factual information, specifications, historical references, values, descriptions, statistics, or related content accompanying visual materials are provided for general informational purposes only and may change over time. Readers should conduct their own independent research and consult appropriate sources or qualified professionals when making decisions based on information presented in this publication.

This publication is independently produced and is not affiliated with, endorsed by, sponsored by, or associated with any company, organization, government agency, institution, trademark holder, or third party unless specifically stated otherwise.

# Table of Contents

# Introduction: Fiscal Policy as Macroeconomic Strategy

Fiscal policy is one of the primary mechanisms through which governments influence macroeconomic conditions. Decisions involving taxation, expenditures, transfers, borrowing, and budget balances can alter aggregate demand, affect the allocation of resources, influence private-sector incentives, and change the trajectory of public debt. Yet fiscal policy is rarely a matter of simply choosing between higher spending and lower spending, or between higher taxes and lower taxes. Each intervention operates within an economy already shaped by inflation, employment, productive capacity, interest rates, private investment, demographic pressures, financial conditions, and monetary policy.

For decision makers, the central question is therefore not whether fiscal policy affects the economy. It clearly does. The more difficult questions concern **magnitude, timing, transmission, sustainability, and tradeoffs**. A policy capable of supporting output during a severe contraction may produce considerably different effects when implemented in an economy operating near capacity. A deficit used to finance productive infrastructure may have different long-term implications from a deficit created by expenditures that generate little additional productive capacity. The same nominal fiscal intervention can therefore produce very different macroeconomic outcomes depending on the conditions under which it occurs.

## The Scope and Purpose of Fiscal Policy

**Fiscal policy** encompasses government decisions concerning expenditures, taxation, transfers, and the financing of resulting budget balances. These decisions influence both the level of economic activity and the distribution of resources across the economy.

At the most immediate level, governments can alter aggregate demand through changes in spending and taxation. An increase in government purchases directly contributes to demand for goods and services. Tax reductions can increase disposable income or alter incentives for investment, employment, and production. Transfers can redirect purchasing power toward particular households or sectors. Conversely, spending reductions and tax increases can restrain demand and contribute to fiscal consolidation.

The purpose of fiscal policy, however, extends beyond short-term demand management.

Governments use fiscal instruments to pursue numerous objectives, including:

- Stabilizing economic activity during recessions or periods of excessive demand
- Financing public goods, infrastructure, education, defense, and other government functions
- Influencing incentives for consumption, saving, labor, and investment
- Redistributing income and providing social insurance
- Supporting long-term productive capacity
- Managing deficits, debt accumulation, and sovereign financing requirements

These objectives can complement one another, but they can also conflict.

A government attempting to reduce unemployment during a downturn may accept a larger budget deficit in exchange for stronger near-term demand. A government facing persistent inflation may instead seek to reduce fiscal support. A government with deteriorating debt dynamics may prioritize fiscal consolidation even when economic growth is relatively weak.

This is why evaluating fiscal policy requires more than observing whether government spending increased or decreased. The relevant analysis concerns **what changed, why it changed, how it was financed, which economic agents were affected, what conditions existed when the policy was implemented, and how the consequences evolve over time**.

The composition of fiscal policy matters as much as its headline size.

Two fiscal packages costing the government the same amount can have substantially different effects. Infrastructure investment, household transfers, corporate tax reductions, payroll tax changes, public-sector employment, and debt-service expenditures transmit through the economy differently. Their effects depend on behavioral responses, implementation speed, import leakage, monetary conditions, productive capacity, and expectations about future policy.

Fiscal policy must therefore be examined as a collection of instruments rather than a single variable.

## Fiscal Policy Within the Broader Macroeconomic System

Fiscal policy does not operate independently from the rest of the economy. It enters a system in which households, firms, financial institutions, governments, foreign economies, and central banks are continuously responding to one another.

One useful starting point is the expenditure identity:

$$\mathbf{Y = C + I + G + (X - M)}$$

where **Y** represents national output, **C** represents consumption, **I** represents investment, **G** represents government purchases, and **X - M** represents net exports.

Government purchases appear directly within aggregate expenditure, but fiscal policy can also influence the other components.

Changes in taxation can alter household consumption. Business tax provisions can affect investment incentives. Government borrowing can influence financial conditions and the allocation of capital. Fiscal expansion can increase imports as domestic demand rises. Public investment can affect future productivity and potentially alter private investment decisions.

The initial fiscal action is therefore only the beginning of the analysis.

Suppose the government increases expenditures during a recession. The immediate increase in government demand may raise output and income. Higher income may produce additional consumption, creating subsequent rounds of expenditure. This process is associated with the **fiscal multiplier**, which measures the change in economic output associated with a change in a fiscal instrument.

But the multiplier is not a universal constant.

Its magnitude can depend on the amount of unused economic capacity, household saving behavior, taxation, imports, financial conditions, the type of expenditure, expectations, and the response of monetary policy. When unemployment is high and productive resources are underutilized, additional demand may translate relatively strongly into additional output. When an economy is already operating close to capacity, additional demand may produce a greater response in prices than in real production.

This distinction becomes particularly important when analyzing inflation.

Fiscal expansion is sometimes discussed as though an increase in spending mechanically produces inflation. That interpretation is incomplete. The inflationary consequences depend partly on whether the economy can expand production in response to additional demand.

If firms have idle capacity and unemployed workers are available, production may increase substantially. If labor markets are already tight, factories are operating near capacity, and critical inputs are constrained, additional demand can increasingly compete for scarce resources. Prices and wages may then respond more strongly.

Fiscal policy consequently cannot be evaluated without considering the **output gap**, productive capacity, and prevailing economic conditions.

The relationship with monetary policy is equally important.

A government may implement expansionary fiscal policy while a central bank is attempting to restrain inflation through tighter monetary policy. Fiscal policy would then be supporting demand while monetary policy is attempting to suppress it. Higher policy rates may offset part of the fiscal stimulus, increase government borrowing costs, reduce interest-sensitive private investment, and alter the eventual multiplier.

Alternatively, fiscal and monetary authorities may respond to a severe contraction in the same direction, producing substantially different macroeconomic dynamics.

Fiscal analysis must therefore consider the complete policy environment rather than treating the government budget as an isolated system.

# Policy Objectives, Constraints, and Tradeoffs

Fiscal policy exists within constraints. Governments can borrow, tax, spend, and transfer resources, but none of these actions eliminates scarcity. Policy instead changes how resources are mobilized, allocated, and financed across sectors and across time.

This creates **fiscal tradeoffs**.

Consider deficit-financed government investment. Borrowing may allow a government to undertake a major infrastructure program without imposing an equivalent immediate increase in taxation. If the investment raises productivity, reduces transportation costs, facilitates private investment, or expands productive capacity, the resulting economic benefits may extend well beyond the initial expenditure.

The debt created to finance that investment nevertheless remains relevant.

Interest must be paid. Debt may need to be refinanced. Future fiscal resources may be committed to servicing existing obligations. If borrowing costs rise faster than government revenues or economic output, debt dynamics can become increasingly difficult to manage.

This introduces the concept of **fiscal sustainability**. Sustainability is not simply a question of whether government debt exists or whether the budget is currently in deficit. Governments can operate with persistent debt and deficits without necessarily encountering a fiscal crisis. The more important issue is whether the trajectory of debt can be maintained given economic growth, interest rates, primary budget balances, revenue capacity, investor confidence, and institutional credibility.

Debt-to-GDP dynamics are particularly important because the burden of debt cannot be evaluated from the nominal debt stock alone. An economy capable of generating significantly more income over time may be able to support a larger nominal debt burden than a stagnant economy.

The relationship between the effective interest rate on government debt and the economy's nominal growth rate can therefore materially influence debt dynamics. When borrowing costs remain below nominal economic growth for extended periods, a given debt burden can be easier to stabilize. When borrowing costs persistently exceed growth, stabilizing debt may require stronger primary balances.

Even then, the analysis cannot stop at debt arithmetic.

Fiscal consolidation intended to improve the budget balance can weaken aggregate demand, particularly when undertaken during already weak economic conditions. Lower output can reduce tax revenues and increase certain transfer expenditures, partially offsetting the intended improvement in the fiscal position. Conversely, delaying adjustment indefinitely can allow interest costs and refinancing requirements to become increasingly restrictive.

Decision makers are therefore frequently choosing among imperfect alternatives.

The same problem appears when evaluating **crowding out**. Government borrowing can compete with private demand for financial resources and potentially place upward pressure on interest rates, reducing some forms of private investment. Yet the strength of this effect depends on economic conditions and monetary responses. During periods of weak private demand and substantial unused capacity, government expenditure may instead support activity that encourages additional private investment, sometimes described as crowding in.

Neither mechanism should be treated as automatic.

Expectations further complicate fiscal policy. Households and firms make decisions based not only on current tax rates and expenditures but also on what they expect governments to do in the future. A temporary tax reduction may generate a different consumption response from a tax change believed to be permanent. A large increase in public debt may influence expectations concerning future taxation, inflation, interest rates, or fiscal consolidation.

Fiscal policy consequently operates through both **current economic flows and expectations about future policy**.

For policymakers and analysts, this means fiscal decisions should rarely be judged using a single indicator. Stronger GDP growth does not necessarily establish that a policy was optimal. A smaller deficit does not necessarily establish that fiscal policy improved economic welfare. Lower taxes do not necessarily produce sufficient growth to offset lost revenue, just as higher government spending does not necessarily produce output gains equal to the amount spent.

Policy evaluation requires examining the counterfactual: **What would likely have occurred without the intervention?**

That question is difficult because the counterfactual cannot be directly observed. Economists instead rely on models, historical evidence, comparative analysis, empirical estimation, and institutional knowledge. Each provides information, but none eliminates uncertainty.

That uncertainty is part of fiscal decision-making rather than a reason to abandon analysis.

The objective is to determine which policy is most defensible given the economic conditions, available evidence, institutional constraints, distribution of risks, and consequences of being wrong.

# Last Thoughts

Fiscal policy is ultimately an exercise in macroeconomic strategy under uncertainty. Government spending, taxation, deficits, and debt cannot be evaluated independently from growth, inflation, productive capacity, interest rates, monetary policy, private-sector behavior, and expectations. The important question is rarely whether a particular fiscal instrument is inherently good or bad. The more useful question is whether the instrument is appropriate for the economic environment in which it is being deployed, whether its transmission mechanisms support the intended objective, and whether its short-term benefits justify its longer-term costs and constraints. The chapters that follow will build on this framework by examining government spending and taxation, fiscal multipliers and output gaps, stabilization across economic cycles, public debt and sustainability, private-market responses, and the interaction between fiscal and monetary policy.

# Chapter 1: Government Spending, Taxation, and Aggregate Demand

Fiscal policy begins with the government's ability to alter spending and taxation, but the macroeconomic consequences extend well beyond the government's own balance sheet. Changes in expenditures and taxes affect aggregate demand, household income, business expectations, investment decisions, employment, and the allocation of productive resources. The magnitude of those effects depends on what the government changes, which economic agents are affected, how the policy is financed, and the economic environment in which the intervention occurs. For decision makers, the important distinction is between the **initial fiscal action** and the broader economic response that follows it.

## Government Expenditures and the Composition of Demand

Government expenditure enters the economy through several channels. The most direct is government purchases of currently produced goods and services. Governments purchase equipment, construct infrastructure, employ workers, contract with private firms, fund research, and acquire services from numerous industries.

Within the familiar expenditure framework:

$$\mathbf{Y = C + I + G + (X - M)}$$

an increase in **G**, government purchases, directly increases aggregate expenditure, assuming other components remain unchanged.

This accounting relationship is useful, but it should not be mistaken for a complete causal model. A $100 billion increase in government purchases does not necessarily increase final output by exactly $100 billion. The expenditure can trigger additional economic activity, displace other activity, encounter supply constraints, increase imports, alter interest rates, or influence expectations.

Composition therefore matters.

Consider two governments that each increase expenditures by $50 billion. One directs the money toward infrastructure construction while the other increases transfers to households. Both measures affect fiscal balances, but their immediate macroeconomic transmission differs.

Infrastructure spending can directly generate demand for labor, materials, machinery, engineering, and related services. A household transfer does not directly represent government purchases of output. Instead, it increases the recipient's disposable resources, after which the household determines how much to consume, save, invest, or use to reduce debt.

Even within direct government spending, the economic consequences vary substantially.

Government expenditure can be directed toward:

- Current consumption and government operations
- Physical infrastructure and transportation
- Education and workforce development
- Research and technological development
- Defense and national security
- Healthcare and social services
- Transfers and income-support programs

The distinction between **government consumption and public investment** becomes especially important when considering long-run economic effects.

Government consumption primarily provides current services or satisfies current public needs. Public investment can potentially increase future productive capacity. Transportation networks can reduce logistical costs. Energy infrastructure can expand productive capabilities. Education and training can affect human capital. Research expenditures can contribute to technological development.

This does not mean that expenditure classified as investment automatically produces a positive economic return. Poor project selection, implementation delays, cost overruns, political allocation, and inefficient procurement can substantially reduce the economic value of public investment.

Decision makers therefore need to distinguish between the **fiscal cost of an expenditure and its economic return**.

The timing of government spending also matters. Fiscal appropriations do not necessarily translate immediately into economic activity. A government may authorize infrastructure expenditures today while actual construction occurs over several years. During a rapidly developing recession, such delays can weaken the usefulness of infrastructure spending as an immediate stabilization instrument even when the projects themselves have substantial long-term value.

The geographic source of production creates another consideration.

If additional government demand is satisfied primarily through domestic production, a greater share of the expenditure initially circulates within the domestic economy. If a substantial portion is satisfied through imports, some of the increase in demand contributes to foreign rather than domestic production.

Capacity constraints can further alter the result.

Suppose the government initiates a major construction program when unemployment is high, equipment is underutilized, and construction firms have excess capacity. The economy may be capable of increasing production substantially in response to the additional demand.

Now consider the same program when construction employment is already near capacity, specialized workers are scarce, equipment is heavily utilized, and material supply chains are constrained. Government demand may increasingly compete with private projects for the same resources.

The nominal expenditure can be identical while the real economic effect is very different.

This distinction illustrates why fiscal analysis must move beyond the size of a spending package. The relevant questions include **what is being purchased, when it will be purchased, where production occurs, whether unused resources exist, and whether the expenditure expands future capacity**.

Government expenditure changes the composition of demand as well as its total level.

That distinction becomes especially important when public spending competes with private uses of labor, capital, materials, and financing. Even when total GDP increases, the composition of economic activity may shift substantially toward government-directed uses.

Whether that shift represents an improvement depends partly on the economic value created and the opportunity cost of the resources involved.

## Taxation, Disposable Income, Consumption, and Investment

Taxes influence the macroeconomy differently from direct government purchases because taxation primarily operates by changing incentives and the resources available to households and businesses.

For households, taxation directly affects **disposable income**, commonly represented as:

$$Yd = Y - T$$

where **Yd** is disposable income, **Y** is income, and **T** represents taxes.

A reduction in household taxes increases disposable income, all else equal. But the resulting increase in disposable income does not necessarily become consumption dollar for dollar.

Households can:

- Increase current consumption
- Increase saving
- Repay debt
- Purchase financial assets
- Hold additional cash
- Change labor or investment decisions

The distribution of a tax change therefore matters.

Households with different income levels, wealth positions, debt obligations, and expectations may respond differently to the same increase in disposable income. A household facing immediate financial constraints may spend a relatively large portion of additional after-tax income. A household with substantial savings and little need for additional consumption may save more of the tax reduction.

This behavior affects how strongly tax policy moves aggregate demand.

The same principle applies to transfers. A transfer targeted toward households likely to spend additional income can have a different near-term demand effect from an equally costly fiscal measure directed toward households with a lower propensity to consume.

Business taxation introduces additional channels.

Corporate income taxes, investment deductions, depreciation rules, payroll taxes, capital gains taxation, and other provisions can influence the expected return from economic activity. Changes in these policies can affect investment decisions, hiring, financing structures, and the location of economic activity.

A reduction in business taxation does not guarantee an immediate increase in investment.

A firm invests when the expected risk-adjusted return on an investment justifies committing capital. Tax treatment is one component of that calculation, but so are expected demand, financing costs, regulatory conditions, available technology, labor availability, and economic uncertainty.

If businesses already possess significant unused productive capacity, reducing taxes may improve cash flow without creating an immediate reason to construct additional facilities. If demand is strong and capacity is constrained, the same tax change may have a larger effect on investment.

This highlights a recurring principle in fiscal analysis: **behavioral responses determine transmission**.

Taxation also affects the supply side of the economy.

Marginal tax rates can influence incentives concerning work, investment, entrepreneurship, saving, and capital allocation. The magnitude of these responses is an empirical question rather than something that can be inferred merely from the direction of a tax change.

A tax reduction can strengthen incentives without generating enough additional economic activity to replace all of the revenue initially lost. Conversely, a tax increase can raise revenue without necessarily producing a proportional decline in economic activity.

Decision makers therefore need to separate two questions:

1. How does the tax change alter economic behavior?

2. How does that behavioral response alter government revenue and the broader economy?

The first does not automatically answer the second.

The structure of taxation matters as well. A government seeking a given amount of revenue can raise it through taxes on labor income, consumption, corporate profits, property, capital income, or other bases. Each approach creates different distributional effects and potentially different behavioral incentives.

Consequently, the macroeconomic significance of taxation cannot be reduced to the overall tax burden. **Tax composition, incidence, timing, expectations, and behavioral elasticity** all matter.

## Expansionary and Contractionary Fiscal Policy

Fiscal policy is often classified according to whether it is attempting to increase or restrain aggregate demand.

**Expansionary fiscal policy** generally involves increasing government expenditures, reducing taxes, increasing transfers, or combining these measures in ways intended to support economic activity.

**Contractionary fiscal policy** generally involves reducing expenditures, increasing taxes, reducing transfers, or otherwise withdrawing fiscal support from aggregate demand.

The classifications are useful, but they can become misleading when treated too mechanically.

Expansionary policy is generally associated with economic weakness. When private consumption and investment decline sharply, government can attempt to offset part of that reduction in demand.

Suppose an economy is producing below potential output and unemployment has increased substantially. Businesses have unused capacity, private investment is weak, and households have reduced consumption.

An increase in government demand can absorb some of those unused resources. Tax reductions or transfers may support household spending. If the intervention raises income and employment, subsequent private expenditure can amplify the initial fiscal action.

The case for fiscal expansion is strongest when the primary constraint on economic activity is insufficient demand and the economy possesses resources capable of responding.

The calculation changes as the economy approaches its productive limits.

When labor markets are tight and production is near capacity, additional fiscal demand cannot necessarily generate equivalent increases in real output. Firms may instead compete more aggressively for workers and inputs. Wages and prices can rise, and imports may increase as domestic supply struggles to satisfy demand.

Under those conditions, contractionary fiscal policy may be used to reduce demand pressure.

A government could reduce expenditures or increase taxes, decreasing the amount of spending circulating through the economy. In principle, weaker aggregate demand can reduce pressure on prices.

The difficulty is that contraction affects real economic activity as well.

Lower government expenditure can reduce revenues for businesses that depend on public contracts. Higher taxes can reduce household consumption or alter business investment. If the contraction is sufficiently large, employment and output can weaken.

Fiscal restraint therefore involves a tradeoff between reducing demand pressure and potentially reducing economic activity.

The appropriate fiscal stance also depends on monetary policy.

If a central bank is aggressively tightening monetary conditions to contain inflation while the government simultaneously implements substantial fiscal expansion, the two policies can work in opposing directions. Fiscal policy supports demand while monetary policy attempts to restrain it.

The result can include higher interest rates than might otherwise have been necessary, greater government debt-service costs, and stronger pressure on interest-sensitive sectors of the economy.

Conversely, during a severe recession, fiscal and monetary policy may operate in the same direction. Lower interest rates can support borrowing and investment while fiscal measures directly support demand.

Decision makers must therefore consider the **combined macroeconomic policy stance**, not merely the fiscal position.

Budget balances alone can also give a misleading impression of fiscal policy.

A growing deficit does not necessarily mean policymakers deliberately adopted expansionary measures. During a recession, tax revenues can decline automatically while unemployment benefits and other expenditures increase. Likewise, an improving budget balance during a strong expansion may occur partly because rising incomes generate additional tax revenue.

This is why economists distinguish between changes produced by economic conditions and deliberate policy decisions.

The distinction will become increasingly important when examining automatic stabilizers and fiscal responses across the business cycle.

Another complication is the difference between **temporary and permanent fiscal changes**.

A temporary spending program intended to stabilize demand during an extraordinary contraction creates different expectations and long-term fiscal commitments from a permanent expansion of government programs. Likewise, a temporary tax reduction may affect household behavior differently from a permanent change in the tax structure.

Duration influences both the economic response and the fiscal cost.

Ultimately, expansionary and contractionary policy should not be treated as ideological positions. They are policy stances whose appropriateness depends on macroeconomic conditions.

An economy suffering from a major demand shortfall presents a different policy problem from an economy experiencing excessive demand and persistent inflation. An economy with substantial fiscal capacity presents different options from one facing high refinancing costs and deteriorating debt dynamics.

The relevant question is not simply whether fiscal policy should expand or contract.

It is **which fiscal stance is appropriate given the economy's position, constraints, risks, and objectives**.

# Last Thoughts

Government spending and taxation provide policymakers with powerful mechanisms for altering aggregate demand, but the headline size of a fiscal intervention reveals only part of its economic significance. Expenditure composition, taxation structure, household and business responses, productive capacity, imports, implementation timing, financing conditions, and monetary policy can all change the final outcome. Expansionary fiscal policy can support output when demand is deficient, yet the same increase in demand can become inflationary when resources are already heavily utilized. Contractionary policy can reduce demand pressures and improve fiscal balances, but it can also weaken output and private activity. Understanding these transmission mechanisms provides the foundation for the next question: not simply whether fiscal policy affects the economy, but **how large that effect is likely to be**. That requires examining fiscal multipliers, output gaps, and economic capacity.

# Chapter 2: Fiscal Multipliers, Output Gaps, and Economic Capacity

The size of a fiscal intervention does not determine the size of its final macroeconomic effect. A government can increase expenditures by a given amount, reduce taxes by an equivalent amount, or transfer the same nominal sum to households and produce substantially different outcomes. The difference lies in how the initial intervention propagates through consumption, investment, imports, taxation, prices, interest rates, and expectations. Fiscal multipliers provide a framework for examining that transmission, but their usefulness depends on recognizing that multiplier effects are conditional on the economic environment in which policy operates.

## The Government Spending and Tax Multipliers

The **government spending multiplier** measures the change in economic output associated with a change in government spending. In its simplest Keynesian form, the multiplier is derived from the marginal propensity to consume:

**Spending Multiplier = 1 / (1 - MPC)**

where **MPC** represents the marginal propensity to consume.

If households spend 75 percent of each additional dollar of income:

**MPC = 0.75**

the simplified multiplier becomes:

**1 / (1 - 0.75) = 4**

Under the assumptions of this model, an initial $100 billion increase in government spending could ultimately be associated with a $400 billion increase in aggregate output.

The mechanism occurs through successive rounds of expenditure. The government spends money, creating income for workers and businesses. Recipients spend some portion of that additional income. Their spending becomes income for other economic agents, who then spend a portion of what they receive.

The sequence diminishes because some income leaves the expenditure cycle through saving and other leakages.

The arithmetic is straightforward. The economic interpretation is more demanding.

A multiplier of four should not be treated as a forecast simply because the MPC equals 0.75. The simplified model excludes taxation, imports, inflation, interest-rate responses, changes in saving behavior, monetary policy, financial constraints, and numerous other mechanisms that can reduce or alter the final effect.

The theoretical multiplier establishes a relationship under specific assumptions. Actual fiscal multipliers are empirical and state-dependent.

Tax changes operate differently because the government does not directly purchase additional output when it reduces taxes. Instead, a tax reduction increases private disposable income, after which households determine how much of that additional income to spend.

A simplified **tax multiplier** can be represented as:

**Tax Multiplier = -MPC / (1 - MPC)**

Using an MPC of 0.75:

**-0.75 / (1 - 0.75) = -3**

The negative sign reflects the inverse relationship between taxation and aggregate demand within the model. A tax increase reduces demand, while a tax reduction increases it.

The absolute value of the simplified tax multiplier is smaller than the government spending multiplier because part of the initial tax reduction is saved rather than immediately spent.

This distinction matters for policy design.

A government deciding between $100 billion of direct purchases and $100 billion of tax reductions should not assume the two interventions are macroeconomically equivalent merely because their immediate budgetary cost is similar.

The tax response also depends heavily on who receives the reduction.

If recipients have a high propensity to spend additional income, the near-term demand effect can be relatively strong. If recipients save most of the additional disposable income, the immediate consumption response will be weaker.

Saving is not economically useless. Savings can support investment and capital formation through financial markets. But the short-run stabilization objective is different from the long-run allocation of saving and investment. A policy designed to generate immediate demand during a recession is evaluated differently from one intended to encourage long-term capital accumulation.

Transfers present similar issues.

Government transfers can produce significant demand effects when directed toward households that spend a large portion of additional income. But transfers do not automatically produce a one-for-one increase in output. Recipients determine how the additional resources are allocated.

Fiscal multipliers should therefore be interpreted as **transmission relationships rather than fixed properties of particular policies**.

A highway project does not possess one permanent multiplier. Neither does a tax reduction, transfer payment, defense expenditure, or infrastructure program. The multiplier depends partly on the policy instrument, but also on the circumstances surrounding its implementation.

That conditional nature becomes particularly important when the economy is operating substantially below or above its productive capacity.

# Output Gaps, Potential GDP, and the State of the Economy

Fiscal policy operates differently depending on the relationship between actual economic output and the amount the economy can sustainably produce.

**Potential GDP** represents the level of output an economy can produce when labor and capital are being utilized at sustainable rates without generating persistent inflationary pressure.

It is not necessarily the maximum amount an economy could physically produce under extraordinary conditions. Rather, it represents a sustainable level of productive activity given available labor, capital, technology, productivity, and institutional conditions.

The difference between actual output and potential output produces an **output gap**.

A simplified representation is:

**Output Gap = Actual GDP - Potential GDP**

The gap can also be expressed as a percentage of potential GDP:

**Output Gap % = [(Actual GDP - Potential GDP) / Potential GDP] x 100**

Suppose actual GDP is $24 trillion while estimated potential GDP is $25 trillion.

The economy has a negative output gap of:

**$24 trillion - $25 trillion = -$1 trillion**

Expressed as a percentage of potential GDP:

**(-$1 trillion / $25 trillion) x 100 = -4%**

A **negative output gap** indicates that actual production is below estimated potential. Such conditions are commonly associated with unused productive resources, weaker labor demand, lower capacity utilization, and subdued demand pressures.

A **positive output gap** occurs when actual output exceeds estimated sustainable potential. This can occur when exceptionally strong demand pushes labor and capital utilization beyond levels that can be maintained without increasing economic pressure.

These distinctions materially change fiscal policy analysis.

When a substantial negative output gap exists, an increase in aggregate demand has room to translate into additional real production. Businesses can increase hours, hire unemployed workers, reactivate unused equipment, and expand output without immediately encountering severe capacity constraints.

Under those conditions, fiscal expansion can potentially produce a relatively stronger real-output response.

As the output gap closes, the composition of the response can change.

Businesses increasingly encounter labor shortages, capacity constraints, longer delivery times, and competition for inputs. Additional nominal demand then has less room to produce additional real output.

The adjustment increasingly occurs through prices.

This is why the same fiscal intervention can be stabilizing in one environment and destabilizing in another.

A large fiscal package introduced during a severe recession may help close a negative output gap. The same package introduced after the economy has already returned to capacity may push demand beyond the economy's ability to increase production in the short run.

Fiscal policy should therefore be evaluated relative to the **size and direction of the output gap**, rather than simply according to the nominal amount of spending or taxation involved.

There is an important complication: potential GDP cannot be directly observed.

It must be estimated.

Economists use labor-market conditions, capital stocks, productivity trends, inflation behavior, demographic data, historical relationships, and statistical models to estimate potential output. Those estimates can change as new information becomes available.

This creates a significant policy problem.

If policymakers underestimate potential output, they may conclude that the economy is closer to capacity than it actually is and withdraw fiscal support prematurely. If they overestimate potential output, they may continue stimulating demand after available capacity has become constrained.

The output gap is therefore analytically useful but inherently uncertain.

Decision makers must combine estimates of potential GDP with other indicators such as employment, wage growth, capacity utilization, inflation, productivity, investment, and sector-specific constraints.

A national output gap can also conceal important differences within the economy.

An economy may have unused capacity overall while particular industries are operating at their limits. A government program concentrated in those constrained sectors can generate substantial price pressure even when aggregate measures suggest that the economy remains below potential.

The **composition of economic capacity** can therefore matter almost as much as the aggregate amount.

## Multiplier Effectiveness, Leakages, and Economic Conditions

The practical effectiveness of fiscal policy depends on what happens after the initial fiscal intervention.

One major factor is **leakage**.

Income created through government expenditure does not remain indefinitely within a continuous cycle of domestic consumption. Portions leave the immediate expenditure stream through saving, taxation, and imports.

Suppose a worker receives additional income because of a government-funded project. The worker may spend some of that income, save some, pay taxes on some, and purchase imported goods with some.

Only the portion that becomes additional domestic expenditure directly contributes to the next round of the domestic multiplier process.

Imports are particularly relevant in open economies. Fiscal stimulus can increase domestic incomes while simultaneously increasing demand for foreign goods and services. The policy may still support domestic activity, but part of the demand effect leaks abroad.

Economic openness can therefore influence multiplier size.

The state of financial markets matters as well.

Government borrowing used to finance fiscal expansion can interact with private credit markets. Under some conditions, increased public borrowing may contribute to higher interest rates or alter the availability and pricing of capital. Higher financing costs can reduce interest-sensitive private expenditure, partially offsetting the original fiscal expansion.

This is one route through which crowding out can weaken the multiplier.

The monetary policy response can be even more consequential.

Suppose fiscal expansion increases aggregate demand while inflation is already above the central bank's objective. If monetary authorities respond by raising interest rates, tighter financial conditions can offset part of the fiscal impulse.

Mortgage rates can rise. Business financing can become more expensive. Asset valuations can adjust. Currency movements can alter trade conditions. Private investment and consumption can weaken.

The eventual increase in output may therefore be considerably smaller than an isolated fiscal model would suggest.

Alternatively, monetary policy may accommodate fiscal expansion during a severe downturn. If interest rates remain low and financial conditions support private borrowing, the offsetting effect can be smaller.

This interaction helps explain why multiplier estimates can vary across economic periods.

Expectations introduce another layer.

A household receiving a temporary fiscal transfer may spend differently depending on whether it views the payment as temporary income, compensation for lost income, or part of a broader permanent policy change.

Businesses likewise respond to expectations concerning future demand, taxation, regulation, inflation, and interest rates.

Fiscal policy can therefore influence behavior before all of the authorized expenditure actually occurs.

Credible announcements of future tax increases can affect current investment decisions. Expected infrastructure investment can influence private development around anticipated projects. Concerns about future fiscal consolidation can alter household and business planning.

Policy credibility can consequently influence transmission.

The duration of the fiscal intervention also matters. Temporary measures can be useful when policymakers are responding to a temporary economic disruption. Permanent fiscal changes alter structural budget commitments and can create effects extending well beyond the original stabilization objective.

Another important consideration is the **speed of implementation**.

A fiscal measure with a theoretically large multiplier may provide little stabilization if implementation occurs after the economic weakness has already passed.

This creates a distinction between the economic potency of an instrument and its operational usefulness.

A large infrastructure program may generate valuable economic activity, but planning, permitting, procurement, and construction can take considerable time. Transfers or changes in existing tax mechanisms can often be implemented more rapidly.

The optimal fiscal instrument therefore depends partly on the expected duration and nature of the economic problem.

Multiplier effectiveness is also influenced by confidence.

During periods of extreme uncertainty, households may increase precautionary saving and businesses may delay investment despite fiscal support. A policy that would ordinarily generate substantial secondary spending can therefore produce a weaker response.

Conversely, a credible fiscal intervention that reduces uncertainty about future demand or financial stability may strengthen private-sector activity.

This is why fiscal multipliers should not be interpreted as mechanical conversion ratios between government expenditures and GDP.

They are conditional outcomes produced by interactions among **economic capacity, private behavior, financial conditions, international trade, expectations, and monetary policy**.

The analytical objective is not to identify one multiplier and apply it universally. It is to determine which forces are likely to strengthen or weaken fiscal transmission under the conditions confronting policymakers.

# Last Thoughts

Fiscal multipliers provide an essential framework for understanding how government spending and taxation propagate through the economy, but they are most useful when treated as conditional rather than fixed. The state of economic capacity, the size of the output gap, household behavior, imports, taxation, financial conditions, expectations, implementation timing, and monetary policy can substantially alter the final effect of an intervention. Potential GDP and output gaps help policymakers assess whether additional demand is likely to generate real production or increasingly encounter capacity constraints, but these measures themselves are estimates subject to uncertainty. Fiscal policy therefore requires judgment as well as arithmetic. The multiplier asks how strongly an intervention may affect the economy; the next question is when that intervention is appropriate. That requires examining fiscal policy across recessions, inflationary periods, and the broader economic cycle.

# Chapter 3: Fiscal Policy Across Recessions, Inflation, and Economic Cycles

Fiscal policy is inseparable from the economic cycle because the appropriate policy stance changes as conditions change. A government confronting collapsing private demand, rising unemployment, and unused productive capacity faces a fundamentally different problem from one confronting persistent inflation, labor shortages, and demand exceeding available supply. Effective fiscal policy therefore requires more than selecting an instrument. Decision makers must assess the economy's position within the cycle, identify the source of the disturbance, estimate how quickly conditions may change, and determine whether fiscal intervention will stabilize the economy or amplify existing pressures.

## Countercyclical Fiscal Policy and Economic Stabilization

**Countercyclical fiscal policy** attempts to move fiscal conditions against the direction of the economic cycle. During contractions, fiscal policy can become more expansionary. During periods of excessive demand, it can become more restrictive.

The objective is not to eliminate economic fluctuations entirely. Modern economies continuously adjust to changes in technology, productivity, investment, credit conditions, trade, consumer behavior, and external shocks. Attempting to offset every fluctuation would be neither practical nor necessarily desirable.

Instead, stabilization policy attempts to reduce economically damaging deviations from sustainable activity.

A significant feature of fiscal stabilization occurs without policymakers approving new legislation. **Automatic stabilizers** cause government revenues and expenditures to respond to changing economic conditions through existing fiscal structures.

During an economic expansion, rising employment, wages, profits, and consumption generally increase tax revenues. At the same time, expenditures on unemployment assistance and certain income-support programs may decline. The budget position consequently tends to strengthen.

During a contraction, the process reverses. Tax revenues weaken as incomes, profits, and employment decline. Eligibility for unemployment benefits and other support programs can increase. The fiscal balance deteriorates automatically, but household income and aggregate demand receive some support.

These mechanisms reduce the amplitude of economic fluctuations without requiring policymakers to identify a downturn, negotiate a response, enact legislation, and implement a new program.

That speed is economically valuable.

**Discretionary fiscal policy**, by contrast, involves deliberate changes in taxation, expenditures, or transfers. Discretionary intervention can be substantially larger and more targeted than automatic stabilization, but it also introduces questions of timing, political negotiation, implementation, and policy design.

The distinction between automatic and discretionary changes is important when interpreting government budgets.

A widening deficit during a recession does not necessarily indicate that policymakers have enacted a large stimulus. Part of the deterioration may simply reflect weaker tax receipts and higher cyclical expenditures.

Similarly, a declining deficit during an expansion may not indicate active fiscal restraint. Strong economic conditions can improve the budget automatically.

Analysts therefore often distinguish between the observed budget balance and an estimate of the balance adjusted for cyclical economic conditions.

This distinction helps determine the underlying **fiscal stance**.

Economic stabilization becomes more difficult when policymakers misidentify the nature of the cycle. An apparent temporary slowdown may develop into a deep recession. Conversely, an economy thought to possess significant unused capacity may recover more rapidly than anticipated.

Fiscal policy can then become procyclical rather than countercyclical.

If stimulus arrives after an economy has already recovered, it can reinforce an expansion rather than stabilize a contraction. If fiscal consolidation is implemented while private demand is already deteriorating, it can intensify the downturn.

Timing is therefore part of the policy itself.

The objective is not merely to choose an economically defensible intervention, but to deliver it while the conditions that justify it still exist.

# Fiscal Intervention During Recessions and Demand Shortfalls

Recessions can emerge from numerous sources. Financial crises, collapsing asset prices, credit contractions, external shocks, declining investment, falling consumer confidence, and sudden reductions in spending can all contribute to substantial weakness in aggregate demand.

When private demand contracts sharply, businesses experience declining revenues and reduce production. Investment may be postponed. Employment can fall, weakening household income and producing additional reductions in consumption.

The resulting feedback can deepen the contraction.

Fiscal intervention can attempt to interrupt this process.

Government purchases directly replace some of the missing demand. Transfers can support household income. Tax reductions can preserve disposable income or alter investment incentives. Assistance to lower levels of government can reduce the need for abrupt spending cuts or tax increases during the downturn.

The appropriate instrument depends on the problem being addressed.

If households experience sudden income losses, transfers may provide rapid support. If private investment has collapsed because firms expect prolonged weakness, public investment can sustain demand while potentially improving productive capacity. If regional governments face severe revenue losses, intergovernmental support may prevent simultaneous fiscal contraction.

The strength of the response should also be considered relative to the demand shortfall.

Suppose policymakers estimate that the economy is operating $600 billion below potential output. A $600 billion fiscal intervention is not automatically required to close that gap. If the effective multiplier exceeds one, a smaller initial intervention could theoretically generate a larger total increase in output.

Conversely, if leakages and offsets produce a multiplier below one, an intervention of the same nominal size may be insufficient.

This makes estimates of the output gap and multiplier jointly important.

Yet recessions also create conditions that make those estimates particularly uncertain. Economic data arrive with delays and are frequently revised. Business behavior can change quickly. Financial stress can alter normal economic relationships. Consumer confidence can deteriorate faster than conventional models anticipate.

Fiscal authorities consequently make decisions using incomplete information.

The costs of underreaction and overreaction may also be asymmetric.

During a severe contraction, inadequate intervention can allow unemployment, business failures, financial distress, and lost investment to persist. A temporary decline can produce longer-term damage if workers lose skills, viable businesses disappear, or investment remains depressed.

This persistence is sometimes associated with **hysteresis**, where a temporary economic shock affects the economy's longer-term productive path.

Such effects strengthen the case for considering more than immediate GDP when evaluating recession policy.

At the same time, large emergency interventions can create lasting fiscal commitments, distort incentives, support activities that would otherwise adjust, or continue after the original emergency has passed.

Program design therefore matters.

Temporary measures should be capable of ending when the conditions justifying them disappear. Permanent structural policies should be evaluated according to long-term objectives rather than adopted inadvertently as temporary stabilization measures.

Fiscal capacity also affects the available response.

Governments entering a recession with manageable debt-service burdens, credible institutions, and reliable access to financing may have greater ability to respond aggressively. Governments already facing high borrowing costs, substantial refinancing needs, or weak investor confidence may confront narrower options.

This is one reason fiscal conditions during expansions matter. Decisions made during strong economic periods can influence the room available for intervention when the next downturn occurs.

A recession does not erase fiscal constraints. It changes the relative importance of those constraints compared with the economic costs of inaction.

## Inflation, Supply Constraints, and the Risks of Excess Demand

Inflation changes the fiscal policy problem because supporting nominal demand may no longer be the primary objective.

When aggregate demand exceeds the economy's ability to supply goods and services at prevailing prices, additional fiscal expansion can intensify price pressure rather than generate proportionate increases in real output.

The distinction between **demand-driven inflation and supply-driven inflation** is therefore important.

Demand-driven inflation can emerge when household consumption, business investment, government spending, and other sources of expenditure collectively exceed available productive capacity. Fiscal restraint can reduce some of that demand.

Supply-driven inflation presents a more complicated problem.

Energy shortages, disrupted transportation networks, agricultural shocks, labor constraints, geopolitical disruptions, and shortages of critical materials can raise prices while simultaneously weakening real output.

A broad reduction in demand may reduce inflationary pressure, but it does not directly produce additional energy, workers, transportation capacity, or raw materials.

Fiscal policy in such an environment involves difficult choices.

Governments may attempt to protect households from rising prices through subsidies, tax reductions, or transfers. These policies can reduce the immediate financial burden on recipients, but they can also preserve demand for goods whose supply is constrained.

For example, subsidizing the consumption of a scarce commodity can lower the effective price paid by consumers while leaving the underlying shortage unchanged. Demand may remain stronger than it otherwise would have been, increasing the fiscal cost of maintaining the subsidy.

Targeting becomes particularly important.

A broad fiscal transfer distributed across the economy can create considerably more aggregate demand than narrowly targeted support for households facing severe hardship. If the objective is to protect vulnerable groups without materially increasing economy-wide demand, policy design should reflect that distinction.

Inflation also affects government finances directly.

Higher nominal incomes and prices can increase certain tax revenues. At the same time, governments face higher costs for wages, procurement, indexed benefits, and public services. Interest expenses can rise as new debt is issued or existing obligations are refinanced at higher rates.

The fiscal position can therefore appear to improve in some respects while deteriorating in others.

Inflation can also reduce the real value of nominal fixed-rate government debt, but relying on inflation as a debt-management mechanism carries substantial costs. Investors can demand higher yields to compensate for inflation risk, maturities may shorten, credibility can deteriorate, and future borrowing can become more expensive.

The interaction between fiscal and monetary authorities becomes especially significant during inflationary periods.

A central bank seeking to reduce inflation may tighten monetary policy by raising interest rates and restricting financial conditions. If fiscal authorities simultaneously introduce broad demand stimulus, monetary policy may need to become more restrictive to achieve the same inflation objective.

This can produce an undesirable policy configuration: fiscal expansion increases demand and government borrowing while monetary tightening raises the cost of financing that borrowing.

The result can be stronger pressure on debt-service expenditures and greater weakness in interest-sensitive private sectors.

Fiscal restraint can operate in the opposite direction. Reducing the fiscal contribution to aggregate demand can lessen some of the burden placed on monetary policy, although the economic and political costs of fiscal tightening remain important.

Not every inflationary episode calls for indiscriminate austerity.

Fiscal measures that expand productive capacity can potentially improve the supply side of the economy even if they require government expenditure. Infrastructure that removes logistical bottlenecks, investments that improve energy capacity, or policies that expand labor supply can have different macroeconomic implications from measures designed primarily to increase current consumption.

This creates an important distinction between the **demand effect and capacity effect of fiscal policy**.

A policy can increase demand in the short run while also expanding supply over a longer horizon. Decision makers must evaluate both effects and the timing between them.

If an economy faces immediate inflationary pressure, productive investments whose benefits will not materialize for years cannot eliminate current capacity constraints. They may nevertheless reduce the likelihood that similar constraints become binding in the future.

Fiscal policy during inflation therefore requires a more granular approach than simply choosing between stimulus and austerity.

Policymakers must identify where inflation originates, determine whether fiscal policy is contributing to excessive demand, evaluate which groups or sectors require support, and distinguish expenditures that primarily increase current demand from those that can strengthen future productive capacity.

# Last Thoughts

The economic cycle changes both the objectives and the consequences of fiscal policy. During a severe demand-driven recession, fiscal expansion can stabilize incomes, employment, and output while reducing the risk that temporary weakness produces lasting economic damage. During periods of excessive demand and constrained capacity, the same fiscal expansion can intensify inflation and force greater adjustment through monetary policy. Supply-driven inflation further complicates the choice because reducing demand does not directly eliminate the underlying production constraint. Countercyclical policy therefore requires accurate diagnosis, appropriate timing, and careful attention to the composition of intervention. It also requires fiscal capacity. Recessions and inflationary episodes eventually pass, but the deficits and financial commitments created during them can persist. The analysis must therefore move from stabilization to the longer-term consequences of **budget deficits, public debt, and fiscal sustainability**.

# Chapter 4: Budget Deficits, Public Debt, and Fiscal Sustainability

Fiscal stabilization cannot be separated from the government's financial position. Expansionary measures that support an economy during a downturn can increase borrowing requirements, while persistent structural imbalances can accumulate into substantial public debt even outside recessions. Neither deficits nor debt are inherently evidence of poor fiscal management, but neither can be treated as economically neutral. Their consequences depend on why the government is borrowing, the cost and maturity of that borrowing, the growth of the economy, the credibility of fiscal institutions, and whether today's fiscal commitments increase or constrain tomorrow's productive capacity.

## Deficits, Surpluses, and Government Borrowing

A **budget deficit** occurs when government expenditures exceed government revenues during a given period. A **budget surplus** occurs when revenues exceed expenditures.

At its most basic:

**Budget Balance = Government Revenue - Government Expenditure**

A negative balance represents a deficit, while a positive balance represents a surplus.

This accounting relationship is straightforward. Interpreting it is considerably more complicated.

A deficit can result from deliberate fiscal expansion, cyclical weakness, structural spending commitments, tax reductions, emergency expenditures, higher interest costs, demographic pressures, or some combination of these factors.

Consequently, two deficits of equal size can represent very different fiscal conditions.

Consider a government that enters a severe recession with a relatively balanced budget. Falling employment and corporate profits reduce tax collections while automatic stabilizers increase expenditures. The government then implements temporary fiscal support to limit the contraction. Its deficit may expand dramatically.

Now consider an economy operating near full capacity that consistently spends substantially more than it collects despite strong revenues.

The numerical deficits may eventually be similar, but their macroeconomic origins and implications are not.

This distinction is why policymakers frequently separate **cyclical deficits from structural deficits**.

A cyclical deficit results from temporary economic weakness and may narrow automatically as economic conditions improve. A structural deficit reflects a more persistent imbalance between government revenues and expenditures that remains even when the economy is operating near its sustainable level.

Structural deficits require particular attention because economic recovery alone may not eliminate them.

Government borrowing finances the portion of expenditures not covered by current revenues. Governments typically accomplish this by issuing debt securities purchased by domestic and international investors, financial institutions, pension funds, central banks, and other market participants.

Borrowing allows governments to shift part of the financing burden across time.

That capacity can be economically valuable.

A government confronting a temporary emergency does not necessarily need to finance the entire response through immediate taxation. Likewise, infrastructure expected to provide benefits for decades can be financed partly through borrowing rather than requiring the current population to bear its entire cost immediately.

Borrowing can therefore facilitate **intertemporal allocation**, distributing fiscal costs across periods.

But borrowing does not eliminate the cost.

Government debt represents a financial claim requiring interest payments and, depending on the structure of the obligation, repayment or refinancing of principal. As debt accumulates, a larger portion of future government revenue can become committed to servicing previous borrowing.

This creates an opportunity cost.

Revenue used for interest payments cannot simultaneously finance infrastructure, public services, tax reductions, or other priorities unless additional revenue is raised or additional borrowing occurs.

The purpose of borrowing therefore matters.

Debt used to finance productive investments capable of raising future economic output may produce a different long-term fiscal position from debt used to finance expenditures that generate little enduring economic return.

This does not imply that every government expenditure must generate a measurable financial return. Governments provide public goods, insurance, security, and services whose value cannot always be reduced to future tax revenue.

For fiscal analysis, however, decision makers must recognize that **the quality and composition of deficit-financed expenditure influence the economic burden associated with the resulting debt**.

## Debt-to-GDP Dynamics, Interest Costs, and Fiscal Space

The nominal size of public debt provides limited information when considered in isolation. A $1 trillion debt burden has very different implications for a small economy than for an economy producing tens of trillions of dollars annually.

This is why analysts commonly evaluate the **debt-to-GDP ratio**:

**Debt-to-GDP Ratio = Public Debt / Nominal GDP x 100**

If public debt equals $20 trillion and nominal GDP equals $25 trillion:

**Debt-to-GDP = ($20 trillion / $25 trillion) x 100 = 80%**

The ratio provides a rough measure of debt relative to the economy's income-generating capacity.

It is not a complete measure of fiscal health.

Two countries with identical debt-to-GDP ratios can face substantially different borrowing conditions because of differences in interest rates, economic growth, currency arrangements, debt maturity, investor confidence, domestic savings, institutional credibility, and the composition of their liabilities.

The dynamics of the ratio are particularly important.

A useful simplified relationship is:

**Change in Debt-to-GDP Ratio approximately equals (r - g)d - Primary Balance**

where:

- **r** represents the effective interest rate on government debt
- **g** represents the nominal growth rate of the economy
- **d** represents the existing debt-to-GDP ratio
- **Primary Balance** represents government revenue minus non-interest expenditure, relative to GDP

The **primary balance** excludes interest payments. This allows analysts to distinguish the government's current fiscal position from the cost of servicing debt accumulated in previous periods.

The relationship between **r and g** can materially alter debt dynamics.

If nominal economic growth exceeds the effective interest rate on government debt, the denominator of the debt-to-GDP ratio can grow relatively quickly compared with accumulated interest. Under favorable conditions, a government may be able to stabilize or even reduce the debt ratio while running a modest primary deficit.

If the effective interest rate persistently exceeds nominal growth, debt stabilization becomes more demanding. Larger primary surpluses may eventually be required to prevent the ratio from continuing to increase.

Consider a simplified example.

Suppose:

**Debt-to-GDP = 100%**

**Effective interest rate = 5%**

**Nominal GDP growth = 3%**

Ignoring other complications, the interest-growth differential is approximately two percentage points. With debt equal to 100 percent of GDP, this differential places upward pressure on the debt ratio unless the government runs a sufficient primary surplus.

The mathematics becomes increasingly consequential at high debt levels because a given interest-rate increase applies to a larger debt stock.

This brings **interest costs** to the center of fiscal analysis.

When interest rates remain low, governments can carry substantial debt with relatively manageable annual servicing costs. When rates rise, newly issued debt becomes more expensive. Existing debt also becomes more expensive as securities mature and are refinanced.

The speed at which higher market rates affect the budget depends partly on the maturity structure of government debt.

A government financed heavily through short-term securities can experience rising interest costs relatively quickly. A government that locked in long-term fixed rates may experience the adjustment more gradually.

Average maturity therefore influences fiscal exposure to interest-rate shocks.

This leads to the concept of **fiscal space**, which refers broadly to a government's capacity to use fiscal resources or increase borrowing without creating unacceptable risks to fiscal sustainability, financing conditions, or economic stability.

Fiscal space cannot be reduced to a universal debt threshold.

A government with deep capital markets, strong institutions, reliable tax capacity, long debt maturities, credible monetary arrangements, and debt issued primarily in its own currency may possess considerably greater fiscal flexibility than another government with the same debt ratio but weaker institutions and substantial foreign-currency liabilities.

Market confidence matters because governments continually refinance portions of outstanding debt.

A fiscal position that appears manageable at a 3 percent borrowing cost can look very different at 7 percent.

Changes in investor perceptions can therefore alter fiscal constraints even when the nominal debt stock has not changed dramatically.

Decision makers must consequently consider not only how much debt exists, but also **who holds it, what currency it is denominated in, when it matures, what interest rate it carries, and how easily it can be refinanced**.

# Debt Sustainability and Intertemporal Policy Tradeoffs

**Debt sustainability** concerns whether a government can maintain its fiscal obligations over time without requiring implausibly large future adjustments, defaulting on obligations, generating severe macroeconomic instability, or otherwise losing reliable access to financing.

Sustainability is therefore forward-looking.

The current debt ratio matters, but so do expected growth, interest rates, future primary balances, demographic trends, entitlement commitments, tax capacity, productivity, and contingent liabilities.

A government can have a high debt ratio and remain financially stable for an extended period. Another government can encounter financing pressure at a much lower ratio.

Context determines the constraint.

One useful way to analyze sustainability is through the government's **intertemporal budget constraint**. Current borrowing creates claims on future fiscal resources. Over a sufficiently long horizon, the government's expenditures, revenues, debt service, and financing must remain compatible with one another.

This does not require every annual budget to balance.

Attempting to balance the budget every year could itself destabilize the economy. During a recession, tax revenues decline and stabilization expenditures rise. Immediately raising taxes or cutting expenditures enough to eliminate the resulting deficit could intensify the contraction.

The relevant question is whether the longer-term fiscal trajectory is credible.

A government can accept large temporary deficits during extraordinary conditions while maintaining a credible expectation that the fiscal position will improve as the economy normalizes.

Problems become more difficult when temporary deficits evolve into permanent structural imbalances.

Persistent borrowing can create a compounding process:

**Higher Debt -> Higher Interest Expense -> Larger Deficits -> Additional Borrowing -> Higher Debt**

This process is not inevitable. Economic growth, fiscal adjustments, declining interest rates, and stronger revenues can interrupt it.

But once interest expenditures become sufficiently large, fiscal flexibility can narrow.

Debt servicing can begin competing directly with other government priorities. Policymakers then face increasingly difficult choices among raising taxes, reducing primary expenditures, borrowing more, or accepting other forms of economic adjustment.

This is where intertemporal tradeoffs become central.

Borrowing allows current taxpayers and beneficiaries to avoid bearing the full immediate cost of government expenditures. Future taxpayers may inherit some of the resulting obligations.

Whether that transfer is economically defensible depends partly on what current borrowing accomplishes.

Borrowing to finance infrastructure that raises future productivity may leave future taxpayers with both additional debt and a more productive economy. Borrowing that repeatedly finances current expenditures without strengthening productive capacity may leave future fiscal resources more constrained without an equivalent expansion in the economic base.

The distinction is not always clean, but it matters.

Fiscal consolidation presents its own intertemporal tradeoffs.

Reducing deficits rapidly can improve projected debt dynamics, but substantial tax increases or expenditure reductions can weaken current demand. If consolidation significantly reduces investment in infrastructure, education, research, or other productivity-enhancing areas, short-term deficit reduction could also weaken future growth.

A policy intended to improve the numerator of the debt-to-GDP ratio can therefore adversely affect the denominator.

This is why debt sustainability cannot be pursued solely through accounting targets.

The composition, timing, and macroeconomic consequences of fiscal adjustment matter.

Credibility also affects the tradeoff.

Governments do not necessarily need to implement every adjustment immediately if investors and the public believe that a credible medium-term fiscal framework exists. Clear institutions, realistic projections, transparent budgeting, and a demonstrated capacity to modify policy can influence financing conditions.

Conversely, repeated reliance on unrealistic growth assumptions or indefinite postponement of known fiscal pressures can weaken confidence.

Decision makers must therefore manage both **current fiscal conditions and expectations about future fiscal behavior**.

There is no single debt ratio at which fiscal policy automatically becomes unsustainable. Nor is there a ratio below which borrowing is automatically harmless.

Sustainability emerges from the interaction among debt, interest costs, growth, primary balances, institutional capacity, financing structure, and market confidence.

The appropriate policy question is consequently not, "How much debt is too much?"

It is: **What fiscal trajectory can this economy sustain under plausible economic and financial conditions, and how vulnerable is that trajectory if those conditions deteriorate?**

That framing forces decision makers to consider scenarios rather than rely on a single forecast.

A fiscal plan that remains stable only under optimistic growth and permanently low interest rates is fundamentally different from one that remains manageable across a range of adverse conditions.

Resilience is therefore an important component of sustainability.

## Last Thoughts

Budget deficits and public debt allow governments to distribute fiscal costs across time, respond to economic emergencies, and finance investments whose benefits may extend across generations. Those advantages do not make borrowing costless. Debt creates future interest obligations, refinancing requirements, exposure to changing financial conditions, and potential constraints on future policy. The sustainability of that debt depends not merely on its nominal size but on the relationship among economic growth, interest rates, primary balances, maturity structure, institutional credibility, and the productive value created by fiscal policy. Decision makers therefore need to evaluate debt dynamically rather than through arbitrary thresholds. Yet government borrowing also interacts with private capital markets, investment decisions, and resource allocation. Understanding those interactions requires turning next to **private markets, crowding out, and fiscal transmission**.

# Chapter 5: Private Markets, Crowding Out, and Fiscal Transmission

Fiscal policy does not operate alongside private markets without affecting them. Government borrowing changes the demand for financing, public expenditures alter demand for labor and capital, tax policy changes expected returns, and fiscal decisions influence expectations about future growth, inflation, taxation, and interest rates. The resulting private-sector response can reinforce the original fiscal intervention or offset part of it. Understanding this interaction is essential because the ultimate effect of fiscal policy depends not only on what the government does, but also on how households, firms, investors, lenders, and financial markets respond.

## Government Borrowing, Interest Rates, and Private Investment

When government expenditures exceed revenues, the resulting deficit generally requires financing. Government borrowing introduces additional demand for funds within financial markets and increases the supply of government securities available to investors.

Under certain conditions, this additional borrowing can influence interest rates.

A simplified loanable-funds framework illustrates the mechanism. Government borrowing increases demand for available savings. If the supply of savings does not increase sufficiently to accommodate that additional demand, the price of obtaining capital can rise.

That price is reflected in interest rates.

Higher interest rates can then affect **private investment** because firms evaluate potential projects partly according to their financing costs and expected rates of return.

Suppose a business is considering an expansion expected to produce a 7 percent return. If financing is available at 4 percent, the investment may be attractive. If borrowing costs rise to 7 percent, the same project becomes considerably less appealing.

This creates a potential transmission sequence:

Government borrowing increases -> demand for financing rises -> interest rates increase -> some private investments become less attractive -> private investment declines.

The relationship is economically important, but it is not automatic.

Financial markets are not closed pools containing a permanently fixed quantity of savings. Capital can move internationally, household saving can change, central banks can influence financial conditions, and financial institutions can alter credit creation.

The state of the economy also matters.

During a severe recession, private investment demand may already be weak. Businesses may have little interest in borrowing even when interest rates are low because existing capacity is underutilized and expected demand is poor.

Government borrowing under these conditions does not necessarily compete aggressively with private borrowers.

The situation can change as the economy strengthens.

When private investment is already robust and capital markets are experiencing substantial demand for financing, additional government borrowing can create greater competition for available resources.

The interest-rate effect of fiscal expansion is therefore conditional on the broader financial and economic environment.

Government debt can also affect interest rates through expectations.

Investors evaluate inflation, fiscal sustainability, monetary policy, sovereign risk, and the future supply of government securities. If markets expect persistent deficits to increase inflation or fiscal risk, investors may demand higher yields as compensation.

The government's financing structure matters as well.

Short-term borrowing exposes fiscal authorities more quickly to changing interest rates. Longer maturities can delay the effect of rising rates on government interest expenses, although newly issued long-term securities may still require higher yields.

Private-sector borrowing costs can also respond differently across markets.

Government securities frequently serve as benchmarks for pricing other financial instruments. Changes in government yields can therefore influence corporate bonds, mortgages, and other forms of credit.

However, the relationship depends on credit spreads, monetary conditions, risk perceptions, and market structure.

Decision makers should therefore avoid assuming that every increase in government borrowing produces an equal increase in private borrowing costs.

The relevant question is whether government financing is occurring in an environment where capital, credit, or productive resources are sufficiently constrained for public borrowing to materially alter private-sector decisions.

## Crowding Out, Crowding In, and Resource Allocation

**Crowding out** occurs when government fiscal activity reduces private-sector economic activity that otherwise would have occurred.

Financial crowding out through interest rates is one mechanism, but the concept extends beyond financial markets.

Government projects also require real resources.

Infrastructure requires engineers, construction workers, machinery, concrete, steel, land, energy, and transportation capacity. Public technology projects require programmers, equipment, electricity, and specialized expertise. Defense expenditures require manufacturing capacity, labor, materials, and capital.

When these resources are underutilized, government demand can bring them into productive use without substantially reducing private activity.

When resources are already heavily utilized, the government may compete directly with private firms.

This produces **real-resource crowding out**.

Suppose the construction sector is operating well below capacity. A new public infrastructure program could increase employment and equipment utilization without significantly disrupting private construction.

Now suppose the same program begins when skilled construction labor is scarce and private development is already strong. Government contractors may need to offer higher wages to attract workers. Demand for materials may increase prices. Equipment and subcontractors may become more difficult for private developers to obtain.

The fiscal intervention can still increase measured government activity, but part of that increase may be offset by reduced or delayed private activity.

This demonstrates why resource constraints matter as much as financial constraints.

Crowding out can also occur through taxation.

If higher taxes are required to finance expenditures or stabilize future debt, changes in after-tax returns can influence labor, saving, investment, and entrepreneurial decisions. The magnitude depends on the tax instrument, affected population, timing, and behavioral response.

Yet government activity can also produce the opposite result.

**Crowding in** occurs when fiscal intervention encourages additional private-sector activity.

Public infrastructure provides a straightforward example.

A transportation project that reduces shipping times can improve the profitability of nearby private investment. Expanded electrical capacity can make industrial development possible. Public research can create technologies later commercialized by private firms. Education and training can expand the supply of skilled labor.

In these cases, government expenditure can increase the expected return on private capital.

The relationship can be represented conceptually as:

Public Investment -> Higher Productive Capacity or Lower Private Costs -> Higher Expected Private Returns -> Additional Private Investment.

Crowding in can also occur during economic downturns.

If weak aggregate demand is preventing firms from investing, fiscal expansion that improves expected sales can encourage businesses to reconsider postponed projects.

A firm may not invest simply because credit is inexpensive. It needs a reason to expect that additional production can be sold profitably.

Fiscal policy that strengthens demand can provide that reason.

Consequently, government borrowing and expenditure can crowd out private investment under some conditions and crowd it in under others.

The distinction depends heavily on **resource utilization, financial conditions, expenditure quality, and the state of private demand**.

This is also why the opportunity cost of government expenditure should be considered carefully.

Every resource directed toward a government project has an alternative use. When the economy contains substantial idle resources, the immediate opportunity cost can be relatively low. When the economy is operating near capacity, that opportunity cost becomes more visible because public and private uses increasingly compete.

The economic evaluation of government spending should therefore consider not only the benefits created by the public project but also the value of private activity that may be displaced.

This becomes particularly important for large, sustained fiscal programs.

A short-term intervention during a recession may primarily mobilize idle resources. A permanent increase in government demand can eventually require a lasting reallocation of labor, capital, and production toward the public sector.

Whether that reallocation improves economic welfare depends on the value created relative to the alternatives that were displaced.

## Expectations, Incentives, and Private-Sector Responses

Private markets respond not only to current fiscal policy but also to expectations about future policy.

A government's announcement can influence economic behavior before taxes change, expenditures occur, or debt is issued.

Businesses make investment decisions using expected future cash flows. Households make consumption and saving decisions partly according to expected future income and financial conditions.

Investors price securities according to expectations about inflation, interest rates, growth, taxation, and fiscal sustainability.

Fiscal policy therefore operates partly through an **expectations channel**.

Consider a temporary tax reduction.

If households believe the reduction will disappear shortly, they may treat much of the additional disposable income as temporary. Some may save it, reduce debt, or smooth the additional resources across future periods rather than immediately increasing consumption.

A tax reduction believed to be permanent can produce a different response because it changes expected disposable income over a longer horizon.

Business taxation operates similarly.

A temporary investment incentive may encourage firms to accelerate projects they already intended to undertake. This can increase investment during the incentive period without generating an equivalent increase in long-run capital formation.

A permanent change in the expected after-tax return on investment may influence a broader set of decisions.

The distinction between **timing effects and additional economic activity** is therefore important.

Fiscal incentives can change when activity occurs without necessarily changing how much activity ultimately occurs.

Expectations about future taxation can also influence the effects of deficit financing.

One theoretical argument, associated with **Ricardian equivalence**, proposes that rational households may recognize that deficit-financed tax reductions today imply higher taxes in the future. They may therefore save the current tax reduction to prepare for those future liabilities, weakening the immediate stimulus.

Strict Ricardian equivalence requires strong assumptions, including forward-looking households, access to credit markets, long planning horizons, and particular expectations about future taxation.

Real economies do not satisfy these assumptions perfectly.

Some households face borrowing constraints. Individuals have different planning horizons. Future tax policy is uncertain. Fiscal burdens may fall differently across generations and income groups. Governments can alter expenditures rather than taxes.

Nevertheless, the underlying insight remains important: expectations about future fiscal policy can change current behavior.

Policy credibility consequently becomes economically relevant.

Suppose a government announces a temporary emergency spending program with clear expiration conditions. Businesses and investors may interpret the resulting deficit differently from a permanent increase in expenditures without a corresponding revenue framework.

Likewise, a credible long-term public investment strategy can generate private investment before the infrastructure is completed if firms believe the project will materially change future economic opportunities.

Uncertainty can produce the opposite effect.

If businesses cannot determine how deficits will eventually be addressed, they may become uncertain about future taxes, inflation, regulation, or interest rates. Some investment decisions may be postponed until the policy environment becomes clearer.

Fiscal policy can therefore affect private activity through uncertainty even before measurable changes occur in borrowing costs.

Incentives matter alongside expectations.

Tax rates influence after-tax returns. Transfers can affect household resources and, depending on their design, labor-market incentives. Subsidies alter relative prices. Investment credits change the effective cost of capital. Government guarantees can change the distribution of financial risk.

These interventions alter behavior because they change the relative costs and benefits associated with economic choices.

For decision makers, this means fiscal policy should be evaluated not merely according to how much money is transferred or spent but according to the **behavioral incentives embedded in the policy design**.

A poorly designed subsidy can encourage excessive investment in activities that remain viable only while government support continues. A carefully designed incentive can accelerate investment with substantial spillover benefits.

Similarly, government guarantees can stabilize critical markets during extraordinary stress, but persistent guarantees can encourage excessive risk-taking if private actors expect the government to absorb future losses.

The fiscal cost visible in the current budget may therefore understate the broader economic exposure.

These contingent commitments are particularly important because they may remain relatively inexpensive during normal conditions and become costly precisely when the economy deteriorates.

Fiscal transmission consequently extends well beyond direct expenditure.

Government policy changes prices, returns, expectations, risk allocation, financing conditions, and resource allocation. Private actors respond to each of these signals.

The ultimate macroeconomic outcome is produced by that interaction.

## Last Thoughts

Fiscal policy affects private markets through financing, competition for resources, incentives, expectations, and changes in economic demand. Government borrowing can contribute to higher financing costs and crowd out private investment when capital and productive resources are constrained, but public expenditure can also crowd in private activity when it strengthens demand or increases productive capacity. Neither outcome should be assumed in advance. The effect depends on economic conditions, the composition of fiscal policy, financial markets, resource utilization, and the credibility of future policy. Private-sector expectations further complicate transmission because households, businesses, and investors respond not only to current fiscal actions but also to what those actions imply about future taxation, inflation, borrowing, and economic conditions. These interactions cannot be fully evaluated without considering the other major institution influencing aggregate demand and financial conditions: monetary policy.

# Chapter 6: Fiscal and Monetary Policy in Macroeconomic Decision-Making

Fiscal policy represents only one side of macroeconomic stabilization. Government spending, taxation, transfers, and borrowing operate alongside monetary decisions that influence interest rates, credit conditions, liquidity, asset prices, and financial expectations. These policy systems can reinforce one another, offset one another, or create competing pressures within the economy. For decision makers, fiscal policy therefore cannot be evaluated solely through the government budget. Its effects depend partly on how monetary authorities respond, how quickly policies reach the economy, and which theoretical framework is used to interpret the resulting tradeoffs.

## Fiscal-Monetary Policy Coordination and Conflict

Fiscal and monetary authorities influence many of the same macroeconomic variables through different mechanisms.

Fiscal authorities influence demand directly through government expenditures and indirectly through taxation and transfers. Central banks influence economic conditions primarily through monetary and financial channels, including policy interest rates and broader credit conditions.

When both policies move in the same direction, their effects can reinforce one another.

During a severe recession, for example, fiscal authorities may increase expenditures or reduce taxes while the central bank lowers interest rates. Fiscal intervention supports aggregate demand directly, while easier monetary conditions reduce financing costs and encourage borrowing, consumption, and investment.

The combined policy stance can be more powerful than either intervention considered independently.

The relationship can be expressed conceptually as:

**Fiscal Expansion + Monetary Easing = Stronger Support for Aggregate Demand**

The opposite combination can occur when policymakers seek to restrain an overheating economy:

**Fiscal Restraint + Monetary Tightening = Stronger Restraint on Aggregate Demand**

Coordination becomes more complicated when the policies move in opposing directions.

Suppose inflation remains elevated and the central bank is raising interest rates to reduce demand. At the same time, fiscal authorities introduce substantial deficit-financed spending or broad tax reductions.

Fiscal policy increases demand while monetary policy attempts to reduce it.

The central bank may respond by maintaining higher interest rates for longer or tightening monetary conditions more aggressively than would otherwise have been necessary.

This creates several possible consequences.

Government borrowing costs can increase. Mortgage and corporate financing costs can remain elevated. Interest-sensitive investment can weaken. Debt-service expenditures can consume a larger portion of the government budget.

The result is not necessarily that fiscal policy becomes ineffective. Rather, part of its effect may be offset by the monetary response.

The reverse can also occur.

Fiscal consolidation can reduce aggregate demand while monetary policy becomes more accommodative. Lower interest rates can offset part of the contractionary effect of spending reductions or tax increases.

This interaction illustrates why policymakers should consider the **policy mix** rather than evaluating fiscal and monetary policy separately.

The appropriate mix depends partly on the nature of the economic problem.

A collapse in private demand may justify broad support from both authorities. A supply shock presents a more difficult problem because economic weakness and inflation can occur simultaneously.

Fiscal authorities may seek to protect household incomes while monetary authorities attempt to prevent inflation from becoming persistent. Policies designed independently can then work against one another.

Institutional structure matters as well.

Central banks in many economies operate with substantial independence from elected fiscal authorities. This separation can protect monetary credibility and prevent short-term political objectives from directly determining monetary conditions.

Coordination therefore does not necessarily mean that fiscal and monetary authorities should operate under a single decision-making process.

It means each authority must understand the likely response of the other.

A fiscal authority designing a large stimulus package should consider whether the central bank is likely to accommodate the resulting demand or counteract it. Likewise, a central bank evaluating monetary tightening must consider the direction and magnitude of government fiscal policy.

The relationship becomes especially important when public debt is high.

Higher interest rates intended to control inflation can materially increase government debt-service costs. This can worsen future fiscal balances and increase borrowing requirements.

That does not mean monetary authorities should necessarily avoid tightening because government debt is expensive to service. Doing so could compromise price stability and monetary credibility.

It does demonstrate that fiscal and monetary decisions can become increasingly interconnected as public debt rises.

An additional concern is **fiscal dominance**, a condition in which fiscal pressures become sufficiently severe that they constrain monetary policy.

If maintaining price stability requires interest rates that create extreme fiscal stress, political and financial pressure may emerge for monetary policy to accommodate government financing needs.

Such a situation can weaken confidence in the monetary framework.

Sustainable fiscal policy therefore contributes indirectly to monetary independence by reducing the likelihood that debt-service pressures become a dominant consideration in monetary decisions.

## Policy Lags, Uncertainty, and Institutional Constraints

Macroeconomic policy operates with delays.

A policy can be appropriate when proposed and poorly timed when its effects finally reach the economy.

Fiscal policy is particularly exposed to several forms of **policy lag**.

The first is recognition.

Economic conditions must deteriorate or change sufficiently for policymakers to recognize that intervention may be necessary. Economic statistics are backward-looking, incomplete, and subject to revision.

A recession may already be underway before the available data clearly establish it.

The second is decision-making.

Discretionary fiscal changes frequently require legislative approval, budget negotiations, administrative planning, and political agreement. The time required can vary substantially according to the policy and institutional structure.

The third is implementation.

Even after a policy is approved, expenditures may not occur immediately. Infrastructure programs can require planning, procurement, permitting, contracting, and construction. Tax changes and transfers can often be implemented faster, but administrative delays can still occur.

The fourth is economic transmission.

After money enters the economy, households and businesses need time to respond. Investment projects are not initiated instantly. Hiring decisions take time. Consumption responses can occur over months rather than days.

These delays create the risk that fiscal intervention will affect the economy after the original conditions have changed.

A stimulus designed during a recession could reach maximum strength after recovery is already underway. Instead of filling a negative output gap, it may contribute to excessive demand.

This is one reason automatic stabilizers are valuable. They begin responding to changing economic conditions without requiring a new political decision each time the cycle turns.

Policy lags are only one source of uncertainty.

Decision makers also face **model uncertainty**.

Potential GDP cannot be observed directly. Fiscal multipliers vary. Household behavior changes. Financial relationships evolve. Economic shocks can invalidate assumptions that previously appeared reasonable.

Even the source of an economic disturbance may initially be unclear.

Weak output could reflect insufficient demand, deteriorating productive capacity, financial instability, or several problems occurring simultaneously. Each diagnosis can imply a different fiscal response.

Forecast uncertainty compounds the problem.

Fiscal decisions are based partly on expectations about future growth, inflation, employment, revenues, expenditures, and interest rates. Forecast errors can substantially change fiscal outcomes.

A debt trajectory considered manageable under strong growth and low borrowing costs can deteriorate quickly if growth disappoints and interest rates rise.

Decision makers therefore should not evaluate major fiscal policies using only a single baseline forecast.

**Scenario analysis** can provide a stronger framework.

Policymakers can examine how a fiscal strategy performs under alternative assumptions concerning growth, inflation, interest rates, unemployment, revenue, and policy effectiveness.

A policy that remains manageable across several plausible adverse scenarios is more resilient than one requiring nearly every assumption to be correct.

Institutional constraints also influence fiscal capacity.

Governments operate through legislatures, ministries, agencies, courts, regulatory systems, procurement processes, and different levels of government. Administrative capacity determines how quickly and effectively policy can be implemented.

A government may possess the financial ability to authorize a major investment program while lacking the institutional capacity to execute it efficiently.

This distinction between **financial capacity and implementation capacity** is important.

Increasing appropriations does not automatically increase the economy's ability to design, approve, and construct productive projects.

Institutional credibility matters as well.

Transparent budgeting, reliable economic statistics, credible fiscal projections, clear accounting standards, and predictable policymaking can influence investor confidence and private-sector expectations.

Fiscal policy therefore depends not only on economic models but also on the quality of the institutions implementing it.

## Evaluating Fiscal Policy Through Competing Macroeconomic Perspectives

Fiscal policy has long generated disagreement because different macroeconomic frameworks emphasize different transmission mechanisms, time horizons, and risks.

A **Keynesian perspective** places substantial emphasis on fluctuations in aggregate demand. When private demand is insufficient and resources are unemployed, government spending or tax reductions can support output and employment.

Within this framework, fiscal policy can be particularly important during severe recessions when monetary policy alone does not generate sufficient private demand.

The central concern is that economies do not necessarily return immediately to full employment through automatic market adjustment.

A **Classical perspective** places greater emphasis on market adjustment, resource allocation, private investment, incentives, and the long-run consequences of government intervention.

From this perspective, fiscal expansion can create concerns about crowding out, taxation, resource misallocation, and the accumulation of public debt.

The distinction is not simply between supporting and opposing government intervention.

It reflects different assumptions about how quickly markets adjust, how households and businesses respond, and whether demand management can improve real economic outcomes without creating offsetting costs.

**New Keynesian approaches** incorporate many market mechanisms while recognizing price and wage rigidities that can prevent immediate adjustment. Fiscal policy can therefore influence real output in the short run, while monetary policy and expectations remain central to the broader macroeconomic response.

Other frameworks place greater emphasis on supply-side incentives.

From a **supply-side perspective**, the structure of taxation and government expenditure matters because fiscal policy can influence labor supply, investment, entrepreneurship, capital formation, and productivity.

A tax policy that improves incentives for productive investment can potentially influence the economy differently from a transfer designed primarily to increase current consumption.

These perspectives are not always mutually exclusive.

A policymaker can recognize that fiscal stimulus may support demand during a severe recession while simultaneously recognizing that persistent structural deficits can create long-term fiscal constraints.

Likewise, concern about public debt does not require assuming that every deficit is economically harmful.

The appropriate framework can depend partly on the policy question and time horizon.

Short-run stabilization asks whether fiscal intervention can reduce unemployment or prevent a collapse in demand.

Medium-term analysis asks how the intervention affects inflation, investment, interest rates, and the recovery.

Long-run analysis asks how taxation, spending, debt, productivity, demographics, and capital formation alter the economy's productive trajectory.

A policy can appear favorable under one horizon and unfavorable under another.

For example, a deficit-financed program can provide strong near-term demand support while creating weak long-term returns. Another program may have limited immediate stabilization value but substantially increase productive capacity over decades.

Decision makers therefore need to separate **short-run stabilization effects from long-run structural effects**.

Economic frameworks should ultimately serve as analytical tools rather than predetermined conclusions.

No single model captures every institutional condition, behavioral response, financial mechanism, or economic shock. Fiscal policy should instead be evaluated using evidence, theory, scenario analysis, historical experience, and an explicit recognition of uncertainty.

The relevant questions remain consistent:

What problem is the policy attempting to solve?

What mechanism is expected to produce the desired result?

What assumptions must hold for that mechanism to work?

What private-sector and monetary responses are likely?

What are the fiscal and economic costs?

What happens if the assumptions are wrong?

For decision makers, these questions are more useful than treating any single macroeconomic school as a universal policy rule.

# Last Thoughts

Fiscal and monetary policy operate within the same macroeconomic system even when different institutions control them. Their interaction can reinforce stabilization, create offsetting pressures, alter borrowing costs, and change the transmission of fiscal intervention. Policy lags, uncertain estimates, changing economic conditions, and institutional limitations make those decisions considerably more difficult than static models suggest. Competing macroeconomic perspectives provide different ways to interpret these problems, but none removes the need for judgment. Effective fiscal decision-making requires identifying the economic problem, understanding the transmission mechanism, considering monetary and private-sector responses, evaluating multiple time horizons, and recognizing the consequences of being wrong. Fiscal policy is therefore not a collection of universal prescriptions. It is a framework for making consequential economic choices under constraints and uncertainty.

# Last Thoughts: Fiscal Policy, Tradeoffs, and Economic Strategy

Fiscal policy is ultimately a problem of economic choice under uncertainty. Governments must make decisions about taxation, spending, borrowing, and stabilization without knowing precisely how households, firms, financial markets, central banks, or the broader economy will respond. Every intervention carries opportunity costs, distributional consequences, timing considerations, and potential second-order effects. The purpose of rigorous fiscal analysis is therefore not to identify a universally correct level of government spending, taxation, deficits, or debt. It is to determine whether a particular policy is appropriate for the economic conditions, constraints, and objectives confronting decision makers.

## No Fiscal Decision Exists in Isolation

Fiscal decisions interact with virtually every major component of the macroeconomy.

An increase in government expenditure can support aggregate demand while simultaneously increasing borrowing requirements. A tax reduction can strengthen household disposable income while reducing government revenue. Fiscal consolidation can improve projected debt dynamics while weakening economic activity. Public investment can increase current demand while potentially expanding future productive capacity.

These interactions make isolated analysis dangerous.

Consider a government evaluating a large spending program. Looking only at the immediate increase in expenditure reveals relatively little about the ultimate economic consequences.

Decision makers must also consider:

- Whether the economy has sufficient unused productive capacity
- How much of the expenditure will translate into domestic production
- Whether private investment will be displaced or encouraged
- How the intervention will affect inflationary pressure
- How financial markets may respond to additional borrowing

- Whether monetary policy is likely to reinforce or offset the intervention
- Whether the expenditure creates temporary demand or lasting productive capacity
- How the resulting obligations affect future fiscal flexibility

The same principle applies to taxation.

A tax increase cannot be evaluated solely according to the additional revenue it is expected to generate. Its effects on consumption, investment, labor, incentives, and private expectations also matter.

Likewise, a tax reduction cannot be evaluated solely according to the amount of disposable income or after-tax profit it creates. The behavioral response determines how much of the fiscal cost translates into additional economic activity.

Fiscal decisions also interact with one another.

A government may simultaneously reduce one tax, increase another, expand public investment, reduce transfer expenditures, and alter borrowing. Looking at any individual measure without considering the broader fiscal package can produce an incomplete assessment of the government's actual fiscal stance.

The same problem arises when fiscal policy is separated from monetary policy.

Government officials may believe they are supporting economic growth through expansionary policy while the central bank is tightening financial conditions to contain inflation. The resulting macroeconomic outcome reflects both interventions.

The **combined policy environment** matters more than any single announcement.

Fiscal analysis must therefore be systemic.

Government budgets, private markets, financial conditions, productive capacity, inflation, employment, international trade, and monetary policy are interconnected components of the same economy.

Changes in one area generate responses elsewhere.

The analytical challenge is identifying which responses are likely to be economically significant.

## Short-Term Intervention Versus Long-Term Consequences

One of the most persistent fiscal policy challenges is balancing immediate economic needs against consequences that emerge over much longer periods.

During a recession, policymakers may need to act rapidly.

A severe contraction can destroy otherwise viable businesses, increase unemployment, reduce investment, weaken household finances, and create lasting economic damage. Waiting for perfect information can allow temporary weakness to become structurally more damaging.

Under those circumstances, accepting a larger deficit can be economically defensible.

The long-term consequences of the intervention nevertheless remain relevant.

Temporary spending can become permanent. Emergency tax provisions can become politically difficult to reverse. Additional borrowing can increase future interest costs. Programs introduced for stabilization can create obligations extending far beyond the economic shock that originally justified them.

The reverse problem occurs with fiscal consolidation.

Reducing deficits can improve long-term debt dynamics, but poorly timed consolidation can weaken an already fragile economy. Lower output can reduce revenues, increase unemployment-related expenditures, and undermine some of the intended fiscal improvement.

The appropriate timing of adjustment therefore matters.

Long-term fiscal sustainability is not necessarily achieved by minimizing every current deficit. Nor is short-term stabilization achieved by ignoring future obligations.

Decision makers must consider the **intertemporal consequences of fiscal policy**.

This becomes particularly important for public investment.

Borrowing to finance productive infrastructure, research, education, or other capacity-enhancing expenditures can create benefits extending into future periods. If those investments raise productivity and potential output, future generations inherit both the financial obligation and the productive assets associated with it.

The quality of investment is therefore critical.

Labeling an expenditure "investment" does not guarantee that it will produce sufficient economic returns. Projects must still be evaluated according to expected benefits, implementation capacity, opportunity costs, and alternative uses of resources.

Long-term analysis must also account for demographic and structural pressures.

Population aging, workforce growth, productivity trends, healthcare expenditures, pension commitments, technological change, and other structural forces can materially alter future government revenues and expenditures.

A fiscal position that appears manageable under current conditions may become considerably more restrictive as these pressures evolve.

Interest rates add another layer.

Debt accumulated when financing costs are low may eventually need to be refinanced under less favorable conditions. Governments that allow debt-service obligations to consume an increasing share of revenue can find that future policy choices become progressively narrower.

This is one reason **fiscal resilience** matters alongside fiscal sustainability.

A government should not merely ask whether its fiscal trajectory is manageable under expected conditions. It should consider whether that trajectory remains manageable when growth disappoints, interest rates rise, revenues weaken, or another economic shock occurs.

Resilience requires maintaining the ability to respond when forecasts prove wrong.

## Evaluating Policy Within the Economic Environment

Fiscal policy should ultimately be evaluated according to the economic environment in which it operates.

There is no fiscal instrument whose consequences remain constant across all conditions.

Government spending introduced during a severe recession can mobilize unemployed resources. The same spending introduced into an economy already operating beyond sustainable capacity can intensify inflation.

Government borrowing during a period of weak private credit demand can have relatively limited effects on private investment. Large borrowing requirements in a capital-constrained economy can produce stronger competition for financing and resources.

A tax reduction can support consumption during a downturn, alter investment incentives during an expansion, or add demand to an already inflationary economy.

Context changes the result.

For decision makers, fiscal evaluation should therefore begin with diagnosis rather than ideology.

The first question is:

**What macroeconomic problem is actually being addressed?**

If the problem is insufficient aggregate demand, the analysis should focus on the size of the demand shortfall, unused capacity, multiplier effects, household and business responses, and implementation timing.

If the problem is inflation generated by excessive demand, the analysis should focus on whether fiscal policy is contributing to that demand and whether fiscal restraint could reduce pressure without imposing disproportionate economic costs.

If the problem is constrained productive capacity, increasing demand alone may accomplish little. Fiscal resources may be more effectively directed toward removing supply constraints or increasing long-term capacity.

If the problem is deteriorating debt sustainability, policymakers must examine primary balances, economic growth, borrowing costs, debt maturity, structural commitments, and the credibility of future adjustment.

Different problems require different frameworks.

The next question is:

**What mechanism is expected to produce the desired outcome?**

A policy should have a defensible transmission mechanism connecting the intervention to the objective.

If infrastructure investment is expected to raise long-term growth, policymakers should be able to identify how the project improves productive capacity.

If a tax incentive is expected to increase investment, the design should materially alter the economics of investment decisions rather than merely provide benefits for activity that would have occurred anyway.

If transfers are intended to stabilize consumption, policymakers should consider whether recipients are likely to spend the additional resources during the relevant period.

The third question is:

**What could offset the intended effect?**

Leakages, imports, higher saving, crowding out, monetary tightening, implementation delays, supply constraints, and changes in expectations can all weaken fiscal transmission.

Policy evaluation should account for these mechanisms before intervention rather than treating disappointing results as unforeseeable afterward.

The fourth question concerns opportunity cost.

**What alternatives are being displaced?**

Fiscal resources are finite even when governments possess substantial borrowing capacity. Capital, labor, administrative capacity, political attention, and credibility are also scarce.

Choosing one fiscal priority means accepting less capacity somewhere else, either today or in the future.

Finally, policymakers must ask:

**What happens if the analysis is wrong?**

Macroeconomic forecasts will never be perfectly accurate. Potential GDP is estimated. Multipliers vary. Interest rates change. External shocks occur. Political conditions evolve.

Good fiscal strategy therefore incorporates uncertainty rather than pretending to eliminate it.

Policies can be designed with automatic expiration provisions, conditional triggers, implementation stages, contingency plans, and mechanisms allowing governments to adjust as new information becomes available.

Decision makers should also evaluate asymmetric risks.

If acting too slowly during a financial collapse could produce enormous permanent damage while modest overreaction produces manageable inflationary pressure, the balance of risks may favor aggressive intervention.

Under different conditions, when inflation is already severe and productive capacity is constrained, the risks may point in the opposite direction.

Fiscal policy is therefore not simply about maximizing expected outcomes.

It is also about **managing economic risk under uncertainty**.

## Last Thoughts

Macroeconomics does not provide fiscal authorities with a permanent formula for the correct level of taxation, government spending, deficits, or public debt. It provides frameworks for understanding how those choices interact with aggregate demand, productive capacity, inflation, private investment, financial markets, economic growth, and monetary policy. Fiscal decisions should therefore be judged within their economic environment and across multiple time horizons. Expansion can be appropriate when demand collapses and destabilizing when capacity is constrained. Borrowing can finance productive investments and emergency stabilization, yet persistent debt accumulation can narrow future fiscal flexibility. Consolidation can strengthen long-term finances while creating substantial short-term economic costs if poorly timed. The central task for decision makers is not to eliminate these tradeoffs, because they cannot be eliminated. It is to identify them, measure them where possible, understand the uncertainty surrounding them, and determine which risks the economy is best positioned to bear. That is the foundation of fiscal policy as macroeconomic strategy.

# About the Author

Roggie "Raj" Clark is an entrepreneur and a 10-year marketing professional with a proven track record in e-commerce and digital business growth. Having built and managed successful online stores with thousands of sales and consulted for numerous marketing clients, Roggie has mastered the intricacies of online marketing, branding, and consumer behavior. He has also written several popular books on digital marketing, SEO (search engine optimization), and programming (HTML, CSS, and JavaScript).

As a former marketing manager at a fintech company—a role he secured through his own marketing and financial expertise—Roggie gained firsthand experience in financial strategy and wealth-building. This journey inspired him to share insights with amateur investors, helping them save money, make smarter financial decisions, and build long-term wealth. Raj currently lives in Maryland with his sister and niece.

www.ingramcontent.com/pod-product-compliance
Lightning Source LLC
LaVergne TN
LVHW050824061126
851857LV00012B/967